THE BEST INDICATORS FOR DAY TRADING

A Guide To Technical Tools, Indicators, Volume Signals And Risk Management For Short-Term Profits

JAMES WILLY

Copyright © 2024 James Willy

All rights reserved.

TABLE OF CONTENT

INTRODUCTION — 9

    Understanding the Forex Market Structure. — 9

    Timeframes and Market Sessions — 10

    The Role of Technical Analysis — 10

    Trading Psychology Fundamentals — 11

    Set Up Your Trading Workspace — 11

CHAPTER 1 — 15

Essential Chart Reading Skills — 15

    Understanding Price Action — 15

    Candlestick Patterns & Formations — 16

    Trend Analysis Fundamentals — 16

    Support and Resistance Levels — 17

    Chart Patterns and their Significance — 17

    Market Structure: Highs and Lows — 18

    Price Action Integration With Indicators — 18

CHAPTER 2 — 21

Moving averages and Trend Following — 21

    Simple Moving Average (SMA — 21

    Exponential Moving Averages (EMA) — 22

Triple Moving Average Strategy	23
Moving Average Settings for Day Trading	23
Trend Identification Techniques	24
Moving Average Crossover Strategies	24

CHAPTER 3 — 27

Momentum Indicators Mastery — 27

The Relative Strength Index (RSI	27
Stochastic Oscillator	28
Williams Percentage Range(%R)	28
The Commodity Channel Index (CCI	29
Momentum Index	29
The Rate of Change (ROC)	30
Understanding Divergence Patterns	31
Momentum-Based Trading Strategy	31

CHAPTER 4 — 33

Volume Analysis for Forex — 33

On Balance Volume (OBV)	33
Money Flow Index(MFI)	34
Chaikin Money Flow (CMF	34
Volume Pricing Analysis (VPA)	35
Volume Weighted Average Price (VWAP)	35
Volume Profile Analysis	36
Volume Spread Analysis (VSA).	36

CHAPTER 5 — 39

Advanced Technical Tools — 39
- Bollinger Bands — 39
- Average Directional Index (ADX). — 40
- Fibonacci Retracements — 40
- Ichioku Cloud — 41
- Pivot Points — 41
- Elliott Wave Analysis — 42
- Market Profile Analysis — 42

CHAPTER 6 — 45

Creating a Multi-Indicator Strategy — 45
- Indicator Combination Principles — 45
- Avoiding Analysis Paralysis. — 46
- Signal Confirmation Methods — 46
- Creating A Trading Checklist — 47
- Back-testing Strategies — 47
- Fine-tuning Indicator Parameters — 48
- Building Your Trading System — 48

CHAPTER 7 — 51

Entry and Exit Mastery — 51
- Identifying entry points — 51
- Exit Strategy Development — 52
- Profit Target Calculation — 52

Stop-Loss Placement Techniques	53
Scaling In and Out of Position	53
Trade Management Rules	54
Position Sizing Strategies	54

CHAPTER 8 — 57

Risk Management Framework — 57

Position Sizing Calculations	57
Risk-Reward Ratio Analysis	58
Maximum Drawdown Management	58
Daily Loss Limits	59
Account Risk Parameters	59
Risk Management Tools	60
Developing a Risk Management Plan	60

CHAPTER 9 — 63

Real-time Market Analysis — 63

Live Market Assessment	63
Trending Market Strategies	64
Ranging Market Approaches	64
Volatile Market Tactics	65
Pre-Market Analysis.	65
Session Trading Techniques	66
Market Condition Identification	66

CHAPTER 10 — 69

Common Indicator Traps ... 69

    False Signal Identification ... 69

    Indicator Limitations ... 70

    Signal Validation Methods ... 70

    Avoiding Over-Optimization ... 71

    Managing Indicator Lag ... 71

    Common Trading Mistakes ... 72

    Developing Critical Analysis Skills ... 72

CHAPTER 11 ... 75

Trading Psychology and Discipline ... 75

    Emotional Management ... 75

    Building Trading Discipline ... 75

    Developing Trading Routines ... 76

    Stress Management Techniques ... 76

    Performance Psychology ... 77

    Decision-Making Framework ... 77

    Maintaining Trading Focus ... 78

CHAPTER 12 ... 81

Creating Your Trading Journal ... 81

    Journal Structure Development ... 81

    Performance Metric Tracking ... 82

    Trade Analysis Methods ... 82

    Strategy Performance Review ... 83

    Learning From Mistakes ... 83

Progress Monitoring	84
Continuous Improvement Process	84

CHAPTER 13 — 87

Advanced Market Concepts — 87

Intermarket Analysis	87
Correlation Trading	87
Fundamental Impact Analysis	88
Market Sentiment Assessment	89
Economic Calendar Integration	89
Global Market Influences	90
Advanced Strategy Development	90

CONCLUSION — 93

The Path Forward — 93

Key Learning Integration	93
A Continuous Learning Approach	94
Strategy Evolution Process	94
Professional development path	95
Long-term Success Principles	96
Market Adaptation Techniques	96
Future Trade Development	97

Introduction

You're about to join the volatile world of forex day trading, where opportunity appear and disappear in hours, minutes, or even seconds. Day trading differs from other trading strategies in that you start and close positions on the same trading day, trying to profit from short-term price swings in the forex market.

Understanding the Forex Market Structure.

The forex market is powered by a huge network of banks, institutions, and retail traders spread across multiple time zones. I've seen how the 24-hour market provides unique opportunity for day traders. Because the market is decentralised, prices can fluctuate quickly in response to a variety of factors, including economic data and market emotion.

Timeframes and Market Sessions

Each trading session has an own personality. The Asian session frequently establishes the day's structure, whereas the London session delivers increased volatility. When these sessions overlap, especially during the London-New York hours, the market usually exhibits its most dynamic fluctuations. Monitoring particular time frames, such as 1-minute and 1-hour charts, will offer alternative market viewpoints. Through my years of trading, I've discovered that understanding numerous time frames provides a big advantage in day trading.

The Role of Technical Analysis

Technical analysis is the foundation of day trading decisions. Price charts provide insights into market psychology and participant behaviour. Moving averages, trend lines, and other indicators are used to decode these stories. Your success in day trading is heavily dependent on how well you comprehend and use technical signals to your trading decisions.

Trading Psychology Fundamentals

The markets will test your emotional fortitude. Fear and greed can impair judgement, resulting in rash judgements. I've witnessed several traders with strong technical ability fail because they couldn't control their emotions. Developing mental discipline takes time; it entails accepting defeats as part of the process and remaining calm during both winning and losing streaks.

Set Up Your Trading Workspace

A well-organised trade workplace improves decision-making efficiency. Your configuration should include many charts with varying time frames and indications. A reputable charting platform, news feed, and economic calendar are all must-haves. The goal is to provide an environment that allows you to digest market information rapidly and execute trades efficiently.

Understanding these fundamentals is the first step on your trading adventure. Each component, from market structure to psychology, is critical to your day trading success. The forex market has several opportunities, but success requires more than technical expertise. It necessitates discipline, lifelong learning, and adaptability.

Through years of market participation, I've learnt that successful day trading requires both technical expertise and emotional intelligence. The foundation you lay today will last your entire trading career. Before moving on to more advanced techniques, be sure you properly understand these basic concepts.

Day trading is more than just making quick profits; it is also about having a long-term strategy to the markets. The abilities you gain now will serve as the foundation for your trading future. Concentrate on understanding market dynamics, honing your analytical skills, and cultivating emotional resilience.

The journey ahead requires focus and perseverance. Begin with tiny roles to learn, gradually increasing your exposure as your skills grow. Every market day provides fresh lessons and prospects for improvement. Your success in day trading will be heavily dependent on how well you understand and apply these fundamental principles.

Let's move forward, building on these fundamentals to improve your trading skills. The following chapter will go over essential chart reading skills, which are another critical component in your day trading journey.

Chapter 1

Essential Chart Reading Skills

Understanding Price Action

Market movement is revealed by price action. Through my years of trading expertise, I've learnt that every price swing contains important information regarding market emotion. You'll note how price changes form patterns that repeat across time frames, illustrating the continuous conflict between buyers and sellers. Price action mastery begins with studying how prices react at critical levels, which indicates where the market may shift next.

Candlestick Patterns & Formations

An in-depth analysis of market psychology can be obtained through the use of candlestick charts. Each candlestick represents four critical price points: open, high, low, and close. I've discovered that certain candlestick formations routinely indicate potential market turns. Strong bullish or bearish candles frequently signify momentum shifts, although doji patterns may imply market indecision. Your ability to read these patterns provides you with significant information regarding potential price trends.

Trend Analysis Fundamentals

Trends determine the market's general orientation. When the highs and lows are rising, it's considered an uptrend; when they're falling, it's called a downtrend. After several hours of chart study, I realised that trends frequently last longer than most traders anticipate. You'll learn how to recognise trend phases - inception, continuance, and exhaustion - which each provide unique trading possibilities.

Support and Resistance Levels

Prices consistently adhere to specific levels. Support levels catch falling prices, whilst resistance levels limit rising prices. These zones frequently emerge where many traders make decisions. I've seen how past support may become resistance and vice versa, resulting in profitable trades. Your success frequently hinges on detecting key levels before the market hits them.

Chart Patterns and their Significance

Markets follow repeated patterns. Head and shoulders, double tops, and triangles - each pattern narrates the ongoing power struggle between buyers and sellers. With practice, you'll understand how these patterns form and what they indicate about future price movement. Some patterns indicate trend continuation, while others warn of possible reversals.

Market Structure: Highs and Lows.

Market structure reveals the big picture. Analysing the sequence of price peaks and troughs provides insight into market strength or weakness. I've discovered that understanding market structure allows you to trade with the current trend rather than against it. Your market structure analysis informs decision-making about position timing and risk management.

Price Action Integration With Indicators

While price action is the foundation, technical indicators provide additional validation. The goal is to use indicators to complement, not replace, price action analysis.

After years of trading, I've discovered that the most dependable signals emerge when price action and indicators align. You will learn how to use these tools effectively, resulting in a more solid trading strategy.

Chart reading requires time and skill. The patterns and signals outlined here occur on a regular basis, although never in exactly the same way. Your quest entails learning to recognise the minute differences that distinguish each trading opportunity. Prioritise identifying straightforward, evident patterns before attempting to trade more complex forms.

This chapter's abilities provide a solid basis for efficiently using technical indications. Strong chart reading abilities allow you to check indicator signals and identify any false readings. Take the time to examine historical charts, observing how different patterns played out. This activity improves pattern identification skills, which are necessary for making real-time trading decisions.

Every trader gradually develops their own chart analysis style. The concepts are consistent, but how you apply them changes with experience. Keep honing your chart reading skills; they'll be the foundation of your trading success. Next, we'll look at how moving averages can improve your technical analysis skills.

Chapter 2

Moving averages and Trend Following

Simple Moving Average (SMA

The Simple Moving Average is a reliable compass in the forex market. In my trading experience, I've witnessed how this simple tool cuts through market noise to reveal genuine trends. SMAs are especially useful in trending markets; the 20-period SMA frequently highlights short-term trends, whereas the 50 and 200-period SMAs reveal long-term market direction. The key is to choose the appropriate periods for your trading timeframe.

Exponential Moving Averages (EMA)

EMAs respond faster to price changes than SMAs. I've discovered that EMAs' responsiveness makes them invaluable for day trading decisions. When the 8 and 21-period exponential moving averages cross, they frequently signal potential trade entries. Understanding how EMAs weight recent prices more heavily will help you trade more effectively.

Moving Average Convergence Divergence (MACD) combines trend and momentum analysis for a powerful tool. This indicator's relationship with the zero line reveals trend direction as well as strength. Throughout countless trading sessions, I've noticed that MACD histogram changes frequently precede significant price movements. You'll learn how to identify divergences between price and MACD, which indicate potential trend reversals.

Triple Moving Average Strategy.

Combining three moving averages yields a strong trading system. The shortest MA reacts to sudden price changes, the medium MA confirms the trend, and the longest MA defines the overall market direction. I've honed this strategy over years of trading and find it especially effective in volatile markets. Your success with this strategy is dependent on selecting the right MA periods for your trading style.

Moving Average Settings for Day Trading

Day trading necessitates precise moving average settings. Fast-moving markets necessitate responsive indicators, and the 5, 8, and 13-period EMAs frequently perform well for intraday trades. Through extensive testing, I discovered that these settings provide timely signals while filtering out market noise.

These settings will need to be adjusted based on the currency pairs you've chosen and the current market conditions.

Trend Identification Techniques

Moving averages are excellent at detecting trends across multiple timeframes. Price remains above or below a significant MA, indicating trend direction, whereas MA slope indicates trend strength. My experience has shown that combining MA analysis with price action improves trend trading performance. Your ability to identify trend phases with MAs will improve your trading timing.

Moving Average Crossover Strategies

MA crossovers provide clear trading signals. Short-term MA crossing above longer-term MA indicates bullish momentum, whereas the reverse indicates bearish movement. After years of implementation, I discovered that confirming crossovers with other indicators reduces false signals. Your trading strategy should include clear guidelines for entering and exiting crossover trades.

Moving averages are the foundation of numerous successful trading strategies. Their ability to identify trends, support/resistance levels, and momentum makes them valuable tools for day traders. The key is to combine moving averages effectively with other analysis methods rather than just using them on their own.

Understanding moving averages significantly improves your market perspective. These tools aid in the early detection of trend changes, allowing you to trade more effectively. Maintain focus on price action while using MAs as confirmation tools. This balanced approach produces more consistent trading results.

The following chapter expands on this knowledge by investigating momentum indicators that complement moving average analysis. Continue to practise these concepts; understanding moving averages provides a solid foundation for advanced technical analysis.

Chapter 3

Momentum Indicators Mastery

The Relative Strength Index (RSI

The RSI provides insight into market momentum and possible price fatigue. During my fifteen years of trading, I've seen this oscillator identify overbought and oversold levels with exceptional precision. You'll notice that RSI levels above 70 frequently imply excessive buying pressure, whereas readings below 30 indicate probable selling fatigue. The main strength resides in detecting divergences, which occur when prices reach new highs while the RSI indicates declining momentum, indicating a likely trend reversal.

Stochastic Oscillator

Stochastic compares the current price to the recent range, showing hidden momentum shifts. This indicator works well in range markets, helping to detect probable reversal points. The fast stochastic (%K) and slow stochastic (%D) lines generate trading signals when they cross. When you combine these signals with support and resistance levels, your analysis becomes more accurate.

Williams Percentage Range(%R)

The Williams%R indicator has similarities to Stochastic yet provides distinct information. Through countless trading sessions, I've noticed that %R often signals reversals ahead of other momentum indicators. This early warning system is especially useful in volatile forex markets.

The indicator's ability to identify overbought and oversold circumstances allows you to timing your entries and exits more accurately.

The Commodity Channel Index (CCI

CCI calculates price deviation from the statistical average, identifying unexpected market behaviour. My experience demonstrates that CCI performs particularly well in trending markets. You will learn to recognise when the market enters extreme territory, indicating probable price corrections. The indicator's sensitivity to price movements makes it useful for detecting both trend continuations and reversals.

Momentum Index

The Momentum Index measures the rate of price fluctuations. Through years of market study, I've seen how this indicator may help identify strong trends and probable exhaustion moments. Understanding how momentum normally leads price can help you make better trading decisions; when momentum diminishes, pricing usually follows suit. This information is crucial for managing your positions.

The Rate of Change (ROC)

The ROC measures the percentage change in price over a given time period. This indicator has been particularly beneficial in verifying trend strength and identifying potential reversals. You will learn how ROC can help you discern between healthy trends and those that are losing momentum. The indicator's simplicity makes it an ideal tool for both new and seasoned traders.

Understanding Divergence Patterns

Divergence is when price and momentum indicators move in different directions. I've learnt from considerable market observation that divergences frequently presage large price reversals. Your ability to identify these patterns early on provides you a major advantage in preparing for prospective trend adjustments. Regular divergence indicates trend reversal, whereas hidden divergence predicts trend persistence.

Momentum-Based Trading Strategy

Successful momentum trading employs numerous indications for confirmation. My trading strategy incorporates RSI, Stochastic, and CCI measurements to eliminate false signals. You will create strategies that incorporate momentum indicators, price action, and moving averages.

This multifaceted technique improves trading accuracy and protects against false breakouts.

Momentum indicators are strong tools in your trading arsenal. They assist spot probable price reversals before they occur, providing you an advantage in market timing. The idea is to understand the strengths and limits of each indicator and combine them to create a comprehensive trading strategy.

These technologies work best when combined with adequate risk management and patience. Moving forward, we'll look at how volume analysis can be used with momentum indicators to create an even more robust trading system. Continue to practise these ideas;

mastering momentum analysis takes time but will pay off in terms of increased trading precision.

Chapter 4

Volume Analysis for Forex

On Balance Volume (OBV)

This theory, which underpins OBV analysis, states that volume leads pricing. Throughout my trading career, I've learnt that OBV exposes underlying buying and selling pressure before price fluctuations become apparent. You'll observe that strong trends usually have a rising OBV in the trend direction. The indicator adds volume on up days and subtracts it on down days, resulting in a running total that indicates the direction of money movement.

Money Flow Index(MFI)

The MFI uses price and volume data to assess buying and selling pressure. I've seen that this indicator frequently predicts price reversals several days in advance. MFI is especially effective for detecting divergences, which occur when prices rise while MFI falls, indicating diminishing buying pressure. The indicator's ability to incorporate volume makes it more dependable than pure price-based oscillators.

Chaikin Money Flow (CMF

The CMF provides insight into the strength of price changes. After conducting thorough market study, I discovered that CMF excels at verifying trend strength and probable reversals. You'll discover that positive CMF numbers indicate accumulation and negative values suggest distribution.

The indicator determines whether large traders favour the current price movement.

Volume Pricing Analysis (VPA)

VPA analyses the link between price change and volume. My years of trading expertise have taught me that large volume at market turning points often indicates strong support or resistance. You'll learn to recognise significant volume patterns, such as high-volume breakouts or low-volume retracements, that indicate probable price direction.

Volume Weighted Average Price (VWAP)

VWAP is an important benchmark for intraday trading. I've seen institutional traders utilise this indicator to evaluate trades execution quality. VWAP is particularly effective for determining probable support and resistance levels.

The indicator's use of both price and volume gives a more full picture of market activity.

Volume Profile Analysis.

The Volume Profile depicts trading activity at various price levels. Through several trading sessions, I've discovered how this tool displays where the majority of trades take place. You will see that high-volume nodes frequently operate as strong support or resistance zones. Understanding the price levels at which most trade happens allows you to forecast future market turning points.

Volume Spread Analysis (VSA).

VSA explains the relationship between price spread and volume. According to my analysis, certain volume and spread combinations frequently anticipate large market moves.

You will learn how to recognise professional trading activity using VSA concepts. The strategy allows you to line your trades with the wise money flow rather than following the mob.

Volume analysis in forex demands a different interpretation than in equity markets. Volume data is obtained from your broker's feed because forex trades are conducted over the counter. For a more trustworthy study, use relative volume changes rather than absolute numbers. Despite the fact that forex markets are decentralised, this approach offers useful insights.

Understanding volume trends will improve your trading decisions tremendously. High volume validates price changes, whilst low volume raises danger flags. Combining volume analysis with price movement and technical indicators results in a more comprehensive trading strategy. These tools allow you to assess the conviction behind market movements.

The next chapter delves into advanced technological methods that supplement volume analysis. Keep practicing these volume ideas; they give critical validation for your trading signals. Understanding how volume supports or contradicts price fluctuations is critical for success.

Chapter 5

Advanced Technical Tools.

Bollinger Bands

Bollinger Bands adapt to market volatility by forming dynamic support and resistance channels. Thousands of trades have allowed me to study how these bands expand during periods of high volatility and contract during periods of consolidation. Prices frequently fluctuate between the top and lower zones, presenting trading possibilities. The middle band serves as a dynamic trend line, with band width indicating potential breakout conditions.

Average Directional Index (ADX).

ADX evaluates trend strength, regardless of direction. My experience has shown that ADX readings above 25 imply significant trends, whereas readings below 20 indicate range markets. You'll learn how this tool helps you avoid trend-following methods in rough markets. The positive and negative directional indicators (+DI and -DI) supplement the ADX by indicating trend direction.

Fibonacci Retracements

Fibonacci levels indicate natural market pause spots. Through years of market observation, I've noticed that prices typically adhere to certain mathematical correlations. You'll learn how to identify major retracement levels (38.2%, 50%, and 61.8%) where trends frequently continue.

These levels are especially effective when combined with other technical indicators.

Ichioku Cloud

The Ichimoku Cloud system offers a broad market overview. This indicator has proven to be quite effective in determining trend direction, support/resistance levels, and market momentum. You will learn how the cloud's leading and lagging components predict future price levels. The system's various components work together to produce high-probability trading signals.

Pivot Points

Pivot points indicate probable market turning points. Through considerable trading, I've observed how mathematically determined levels may properly identify support and resistance.

You will learn to calculate daily, weekly, and monthly pivot points for various trading timeframes. These levels are especially helpful when several time frame pivot points coincide.

Elliott Wave Analysis

Elliott Wave theory explains market psychology through price patterns. My work demonstrates how markets move in predictable waves, driven by human behaviour. You'll learn how to recognise impulsive and corrective waves, which will help you predict market direction.

Understanding wave patterns greatly enhances your entry and departure timing.

Market Profile Analysis:

Market Profile shows price dispersion over time. Through extensive research, I discovered how this instrument displays market acceptance and rejection of pricing levels. You will learn how price distribution patterns predict probable market movements. The program excels at spotting value locations where prices tend to rebound.

These advanced tools require a more in-depth understanding than simple indications. Their strength stems from their ability to work together efficiently. For example, Bollinger Bands work well with ADX because strong trends frequently hit the bands while ADX climbs.

Understanding these links increases your trading performance.

Advanced technical analysis requires time and practice. Each tool provides unique insights, but their entire value is shown when utilised together. Concentrate on mastering one tool at a time before expanding your analysis. This meticulous strategy develops long-term trading expertise.

Moving forward, we'll look at how to integrate these advanced tools into a cohesive trading strategy. Continue to explore these principles; they serve as the foundation for expert market analysis. Understanding why these technologies operate is critical to success.

These tools are as sophisticated as the markets themselves. However, with good research and application, they can become valuable allies in your trading adventure. Next, we'll look at how these sophisticated tools can be used to develop effective multi-indicator strategies.

Chapter 6

Creating a Multi-Indicator Strategy

Indicator Combination Principles

Understanding the particular qualities of each indication is essential for combining them. Through comprehensive market investigation, I determined that complimentary indicators produce stronger signals than similar ones. Combining trend-following indicators and momentum tools will provide you with more insight. Moving averages can be used to determine trend direction, RSI to measure momentum, and volume analysis to confirm.

Avoiding Analysis Paralysis.

More indicators do not guarantee better trading decisions. My years of experience have taught me that simplicity usually outperforms complication. Three to four carefully chosen indicators will provide considerable market knowledge. Each indicator should have a specific purpose in your approach, such as identifying trends, verifying momentum, or validating volume.

Signal Confirmation Methods

Strong trading signals are often aligned across numerous indicators. I've found that the most accurate trades happen when price movement, trend indicators, and momentum tools all point in the same direction. You will learn to prioritise signals and understand which indications are more important in different market scenarios.

Creating A Trading Checklist

A systematic strategy turns analysis into action. Through several trading sessions, I've honed my checklist to record key decision points. Your checklist may include trend direction from EMAs, momentum confirmation from RSI, and volume validation from OBV. This organised technique avoids emotional trading judgements.

Back-testing Strategies

Back-testing indicates strategy efficiency under various market conditions. I've discovered that thorough testing necessitates analysing both successful and losing trades. You'll learn how to evaluate your strategy's performance using metrics like as win rate, profit factor, and maximum drawdown. This analysis helps to improve entry and exit rules.

Fine-tuning Indicator Parameters

Default indicator settings rarely produce optimal results. Through systematic testing, I discovered that changing the parameters to meet your trading timeframe enhances signal quality. You will learn how to change indicator intervals while keeping them reliable. Small modifications frequently result in large profits in signal accuracy.

Building Your Trading System

A complete trading system connects numerous components seamlessly. Years of refining have taught me that good systems strike a balance between complexity and practicality. Your system should have explicit rules for entry and exit, position sizing, and risk management. The objective is to create rules that are effective in a variety of market scenarios.

Creating a multi-indicator strategy demands patience and ongoing modification. Each market phase brings new insights into indicator behaviour and relationships. Instead of looking for the exact mix, focus on understanding how different indications compliment one another.

The most effective methods emerge from thorough observation and adjustment. Consider which indicator combinations perform best in trending versus range markets. Your plan should respond to changing market conditions while adhering to consistent risk management standards.

Moving forward, we will look at particular entry and exit strategies based on multi-indicator indications. Keep testing and improving your approach; strategy development never ends. Success comes from consistently changing your approach to market changes.

Chapter 7

Entry and Exit Mastery

Identifying entry points

Precise entries distinguish between profitable and failed transactions. Through numerous trading hours, I've learnt that powerful entry positions indicate a convergence of multiple technical elements. You'll observe that price reacts most strongly when trend, momentum, and support/resistance all align. Strong entrances necessitate patience; the market provides clear settings when you stop forcing trades.

Exit Strategy Development.

Exit strategies require as much consideration as inputs. My trading experience has shown that fixed exit levels reduce emotional decision-making during trades. You'll learn how to set numerous profit objectives and close partial positions as the market swings in your favour. This technique ensures revenues while allowing winners to run.

Profit Target Calculation:

Setting logical profit targets necessitates technical and mathematical analysis. After years of trading, I discovered that past swing points and fibonacci extensions produce accurate target levels. You will learn how to evaluate risk-reward ratios to ensure long-term profitability. Each aim should correspond to key technological levels.

Stop-Loss Placement Techniques

Strategic stop-loss placement preserves cash while allowing trades to breathe. I've observed that effective stops exist outside of usual market noise but within acceptable risk limitations. Your stop-loss judgements should take into account volatility levels and recent price structure. Placing stops just beyond important support or resistance levels frequently avoids premature exit.

Scaling In and Out of Position

Position scaling adds intricacy to your trading strategy. Through market observation, I've witnessed how scaling into positions decreases entry risk while scaling out ensures consistent profits. You will learn how to build on successful positions while taking sensible risks. This strategy maximises lucrative trades while limiting exposure significantly.

Trade Management Rules

Active trade management converts good setups into superior outcomes. My experience has shown that good management standards avoid emotional decisions amid market turbulence. You will create parameters for shifting stops to breakeven, taking partial profits, and modifying position size. These guidelines ensure consistency in your trading strategy.

Position Sizing Strategies

Position sizing has a direct impact on trading success. After much testing, I discovered that regular position sizing promotes consistent account growth. Your position sizes should account for both market volatility and current account balance. This dynamic technique adjusts transaction size based on market conditions and recent results.

Managing trading involves both technical expertise and emotional control. Each market fluctuation tests your capacity to adhere to predetermined plans. The most successful traders stick to their rules, even when emotions force them to deviate.

Mastering entry and exits requires time and practice. Concentrate on tracking your trades and analysing the outcomes. Your trading journal becomes extremely useful for finding patterns in both successful and bad trades. This study will inform future changes to your entry and departure strategy.

The following chapter will look at the risk management framework, which serves as the foundation for all trading choices. Continue to practise these entry and exit strategies. Proficiency is achieved via regular application and careful study of findings.

Chapter 8

Risk Management Framework

Position Sizing Calculations

Proper position sizing is the cornerstone of risk management. Throughout my trading career, I've discovered that constant position sizing reduces catastrophic losses. You will learn how to compute position sizes using your account equity and risk tolerance. The formula starts with estimating your risk each trades, which is normally 1-2% of your account value, and then calculating lot size based on your stop-loss distance.

Risk-Reward Ratio Analysis

The risk-reward ratio determines long-term profitability. The markets have taught me that having at least a 1:2 risk-reward ratio promotes constant account growth. You'll understand how to balance potential profit with early risk. This research helps you avoid low-probability trades and focus your resources on higher-quality possibilities.

Maximum Drawdown Management.

Controlling drawdowns safeguards your trading capital. My experience has shown that restricting maximum drawdowns to 20% of account equity improves trading lifespan. You'll learn how to reduce recurrent losses using correct position sizing and correlation analysis.

Monitoring drawdowns helps you determine when to reduce position sizes or take a trading break.

Daily Loss Limits

Daily loss limits protect against emotionally driven trading decisions. Through years of market involvement, I've seen how severe daily restrictions deter compulsive recovery attempts. Your daily risk limit could be 3–5% of account equity. Once reached, withdrawing from trading eliminates further losses amid unfavourable conditions.

Account Risk Parameters

Setting explicit risk parameters governs all trading decisions. I've discovered that effective traders follow tight criteria regarding total exposure and correlation risk. You will create guidelines for maximum open positions, sector exposure, and currency pair correlations. These settings provide a safety net for your trading activity.

Risk Management Tools

Technology improves risk management efficacy. Throughout my trading career, I've used a variety of risk-management methods. You will investigate position calculators, correlation matrices, and risk analysis tools. These tools assist in maintaining disciplined trading within your set limitations.

Developing a Risk Management Plan

A comprehensive risk management plan brings together all risk control elements. I've learnt from vast market experience that written plans promote adherence to risk management guidelines. Your strategy should include position sizing guidelines, maximum exposure limits, and loss recovery processes. This defined strategy prevents emotions from overpowering sound risk management practices.

Risk management necessitates ongoing monitoring and adjustment. Markets change, and your risk management strategy must adapt accordingly. The goal remains consistent: preserve trade capital while maximising earnings. Successful traders prioritise risk management above finding excellent entry locations.

Many traders struggle with the psychological aspects of risk management. Following rigorous guidelines when markets are moving against you requires discipline and emotional control. Your success is heavily reliant on following these guidelines during challenging market situations.

Moving forward, we will look at real-time market analysis techniques. Continue to refine your risk management strategy; it is the cornerstone for long-term trading success. Without appropriate risk management, even the strongest trading system will fail.

Chapter 9

Real-time Market Analysis

Live Market Assessment

Real-time analysis necessitates a quick and detailed assessment of market conditions. Through my significant trading experience, I've created strategies for quickly assessing price action, volume, and indication signals. You'll learn approaches for detecting high-probability scenarios as they emerge. The objective is to quickly synthesise various data sets and make unambiguous trading decisions.

Trending Market Strategies

Trading trends boosts your chances of success. My experience in the markets has proven that powerful trends frequently last longer than most traders anticipate. You will learn to recognise trend features such as steady higher highs and lows in uptrends and persistent lower highs and lows in downtrends. Momentum indicators serve to confirm trend strength and probable exhaustion points.

Ranging Market Approaches

Range-bound markets require different techniques than trending markets. After several trading sessions, I discovered that oscillators excel at identifying range extremes. You will learn how to identify range boundaries and probable breakout locations. Support and resistance levels become critical reference points during range situations.

Volatile Market Tactics

Volatile markets offer both opportunities and risks. My experience indicates that reducing position sizes while retaining wider stops aids in navigating unpredictable environments. You'll learn how to alter your trading strategy as volatility spikes. During times of high volatility, price activity frequently outperforms indicators.

Pre-Market Analysis.

Preparation before the market opens establishes the foundation for daily success. I've discovered that analysing higher timeframes and recognising significant levels prior enhances trading decisions. You will develop processes for analysing overnight fluctuations, monitoring economic calendars, and noting noteworthy price levels. This preparation gives context to intraday judgements.

Session Trading Techniques

Each trading session has distinct characteristics. Years of observation have shown me that Asian sessions frequently build ranges that European and American sessions do not. You will learn how to adjust your trading strategy for different market sessions. Volume and volatility patterns vary regularly between sessions, presenting distinct opportunities.

Market Condition Identification

Recognising existing market conditions governs strategy choices. My analysis focusses on swiftly determining whether markets are trending, ranging, or transitioning. You'll learn how to identify condition changes using price action and indicator behaviour. This competence allows you to avoid using trending methods in varying markets and vice versa.

Real-time analysis necessitates constant focus and rapid decision-making. The marketplaces change frequently, necessitating adaptability in your approach. Maintain objectivity despite market swings. Emotional detachment enhances analytical quality and trading decisions.

Preparation and practice lead to success in real-time analytics. Daily market review improves pattern recognition skills, which are necessary for speedy decision-making. Long-term success is determined by your capacity to adjust techniques in response to current events.

The following chapter discusses frequent indication traps to avoid. Keep honing your real-time analysis skills; they are the foundation of consistent trading performance. Markets offer limitless learning opportunities for those who remain vigilant and flexible.

Chapter 10

Common Indicator Traps

False Signal Identification

False signals challenge every trader's discipline. With vast market expertise, I've learnt to distinguish between genuine and false indicator signals. You'll learn to recognise when indications may mislead, especially during low-volume periods or during important news events. Real signals frequently demonstrate alignment across various timeframes and indicators.

Indicator Limitations

Understanding indicator limits improves trading decisions. My years of research have demonstrated how each indicator fails in various market conditions. You'll see why trend indicators lag during quick market moves and oscillators produce early alerts during strong trends. This information allows you to avoid trades based on unreliable signals.

Signal Validation Methods

Signal validation differentiates profitable trades from costly ones. Through numerous market hours, I've established methodical methods for confirming indicator signals. You will learn how to cross-reference multiple indicators, analyse volume trends, and check higher timeframes. Strong trades generally demonstrate validation from a variety of analytical tools.

Avoiding Over-Optimization.

Over-optimization leads to false back-testing results. My experience suggests that overly optimised indicators frequently fail in live trading. You will learn how to strike a compromise between indicator sensitivity and reliability. Testing across market situations avoids indicators from being overfitted to specific market stages.

Managing Indicator Lag

Indicator lag impacts all technological gadgets. Through extensive market research, I discovered solutions to compensate for this inherent delay. You will learn ways for anticipating signals before they fully materialise. Price activity typically precedes indicator fluctuations, offering early indications of potential signals.

Common Trading Mistakes:

Trading blunders are repeated over generations of traders. My observations reveal that the majority of errors are caused by misunderstanding indication signals. You'll learn how to avoid typical errors such as trading against strong trends, ignoring volume confirmation, and relying too heavily on individual indicators. Success comes from learning from others' errors.

Developing Critical Analysis Skills

Critical analysis converts information into profitable decisions. Through years of trading, I've created frameworks for objectively interpreting indicator indications. You will learn how to challenge indicator readings and seek confirmation before trading. This analytical technique enhances trading success over time.

Even experienced traders can fall victim to indicator traps on occasion. The aim is to minimise their impact through proper analysis and risk management. Each incorrect signal teaches us how to make better trading selections in the future. Learning from these experiences will help you progress as a trader.

These hurdles determine each trader's journey. Understand why indicators fail under specific settings. Your success is mostly dependent on avoiding common pitfalls and maximising dependable signals. Markets are continually changing, necessitating ongoing modification of indication interpretation.

Moving further, we will look at trading mentality and discipline. Continue to examine these indicator traps; being aware of potential pitfalls helps traders make better selections. Understanding the indicator's strengths and weaknesses is essential for success.

Chapter 11

Trading Psychology and Discipline.

Emotional Management

Trading psychology has a greater impact on long-term success than technical skills. Having spent decades in the market, I've seen how emotions drive the majority of trading mistakes. You'll discover how to maintain emotional equilibrium when winning and losing trades. Strong emotions impair judgement, leading to rash conclusions that vary from tried-and-true techniques.

Building Trading Discipline

Trading discipline grows with constant practice and self-awareness. My experience has shown that established trading rules improve discipline amid market stress. You'll learn how to stick to your trading strategy in the face of strong emotions. Discipline entails completing valid setups even after losses and avoiding trades that do not fit your criteria.

Developing Trading Routines

Structured procedures improve trading performance greatly. After years of practice, I discovered that continuous pre-market preparation decreases emotional trading. You will set up daily routines for market analysis, trading preparation, and performance evaluation. These practices result in a professional attitude to trading activities.

Stress Management Techniques

Market stress impacts each trader differently. My trading experience has taught me a variety of strategies for keeping mental clarity under pressure. You will learn how to manage stress during volatile market situations. Deep breathing, regular breaks, and physical activity all aid with emotional equilibrium.

Performance Psychology

Peak performance necessitates excellent psychological conditions. Through extensive research on great traders, I've uncovered essential mental characteristics that enable consistent outcomes. You will learn how to retain attention, manage fatigue, and stay confident without becoming overconfident. Mental preparation is equally vital as technical analysis.

Decision-Making Framework

Clear decision frames minimise emotional interference. My trading strategy is based on systematic decision processes rather than gut feelings. You will develop organised procedures for analysing trade setups, managing positions, and executing exits. This framework ensures stability amid difficult market situations.

Maintaining Trading Focus

Focus determines trading effectiveness. Through several trading sessions, I've learnt tactics for staying focused during market hours. You will learn how to avoid distractions and keep current on market trends. Sharp attention enhances pattern recognition and trade timing.

Trading psychology distinguishes successful from unsuccessful traders. Technical talents are meaningless without adequate psychological preparation. Each trading day tries your emotional discipline and mental fortitude. Your success is heavily reliant on psychological toughness during challenging market conditions.

The psychological challenges get more complex as trading accounts rise in size. Small account traders experience fear and greed, and large account managers confront higher responsibility stress. These issues necessitate ongoing psychological adjustment and progress.

Moving forward, we will look at how to create efficient trading journals. Continue to improve your psychological talents; they define your capacity to implement tactics consistently. Success is achieved by mastering both the technical and psychological components of trading.

Chapter 12

Creating Your Trading Journal

Journal Structure Development

A well-organised trading journal records critical information for improvement. Years of documentation have allowed me to modify journal forms to capture both technical and psychological factors. You will create templates for documenting entry reasons, departure decisions, and market conditions. Effective journals strike a balance between technical detail and practicality.

Performance Metric Tracking

Data drives trading improvements. My trading progressed quickly after I started regularly tracking key performance metrics. You'll learn how to track key performance metrics such as win rate, average win/loss size, and maximum drawdown. These measurements highlight patterns in your trading performance that might otherwise go undiscovered.

Trade Analysis Methods

Detailed trade research reveals potential areas for development. Through a methodical review, I discovered tiny trends in both successful and unsuccessful trades. You'll learn ways for analysing trade screenshots, market conditions, and your emotional state during trading. This analysis constantly refines your trading strategy.

Strategy Performance Review

Regular strategy evaluations sustain trading effectiveness. I learnt how techniques succeed in different market scenarios by carefully documenting them. You will learn how to evaluate strategy performance, determine when revisions are required, and track strategy changes. This technique ensures that your trading strategy adapts to market developments.

Learning From Mistakes

Trading blunders offer important learning opportunities. My most important growth came from carefully analysing losing trades. You will design techniques for categorising trade errors, determining their root causes, and devising specific improvement strategies. Each mistake serves as a learning opportunity for future trade.

Progress Monitoring

Tracking progress encourages continuous improvement. Through persistent journaling, I've seen modest skill progress translate into major performance profits. You'll set benchmarks for monitoring trading progress, ranging from simple metrics like win rate to more complicated measurements like risk-adjusted returns. Regular progress reviews keep the focus on long-term growth.

Continuous Improvement Process

Trading journals help traders improve their skills over time. My experience suggests that systematic review and adjustment result in consistent performance profits. You will design mechanisms for regular trade reviews, strategy refining, and skill improvement. This systematic technique speeds up trading mastery.

Journaling demands attention and regularity. Many traders start notebooks but abandon them during busy or difficult times. Your devotion to frequent recordkeeping distinguishes serious traders from inexperienced ones. Each diary post expands your trading knowledge base.

The most beneficial insights are frequently profit from analysing numerous trades over time. Concentrate on discovering trends in your trading behaviour and market responses. Your journal gains value as entries accumulate, exposing long-term patterns and tendencies.

Next, we'll look at sophisticated market concepts. Maintain your trading log; it will serve as both a teacher and a guide on your trading experience. Success leaves clues, and your journal helps you find them.

Chapter 13

Advanced Market Concepts.

Intermarket Analysis.

Currency pairs interact in intricate ways with other financial markets. I've mapped links between forex, commodities, bonds, and equities after thorough observation. You'll learn how gold prices frequently influence certain currencies, while oil prices affect others. When properly understood, these relationships can lead to trading possibilities.

Correlation Trading

Currency correlation patterns provide a distinct trading perspective. My findings show how correlation knowledge helps portfolio risk management.

You'll learn how to find pairs that are strongly and adversely associated. Understanding the typical price correlations of correlated pairings, as well as recognising when these links momentarily break down, is required for trading.

Fundamental Impact Analysis

Technical analysis is most effective when combined with fundamental elements. Through years of trading, I've seen how economic data affects currency fluctuations. You will learn how to incorporate fundamental analysis into your technical trading method. Major economic releases frequently result in big price changes, which technical indicators can help navigate.

Market Sentiment Assessment

Market sentiment determines short-term price changes. My experience demonstrates that knowing crowd psychology helps traders make better decisions. You'll create ways for determining market sentiment using commitment of traders reports, positioning data, and sentiment indicators. This study helps to detect probable market turning points.

Economic Calendar Integration

Economic events influence market movements. Through meticulous tracking, I've discovered how different news releases affect various currency pairs. You will develop trading strategies based on key economic announcements. Understanding the impact of events aids risk management during times of high news volatility.

Global Market Influences:

Global events have an impact on currency relationships. My observations highlight how political developments, central bank policies, and economic trends influence FX markets. You'll learn how to keep track of worldwide variables that affect the currency pairings you trade. International awareness increases the quality of trading decisions.

Advanced Strategy Development.

In forex markets, strategy evolution is never-ending. Through constant refinement, I've established approaches for adapting strategy to shifting market situations. You'll learn how to optimise your plan by introducing new aspects while sticking to tried-and-true tactics. Advanced techniques use various analytical kinds to make sound trading judgements.

Markets are always evolving, requiring traders to adapt. Instead of looking for ideal indicators, focus on understanding wider market effects.

Your performance is mostly dependent on integrating multiple analysis types into logical trading strategies.

Advanced trading necessitates the synthesis of numerous information sources. Technical indicators perform best when supported by intermarket analysis and fundamental considerations. Understanding these complicated links will give you an edge in trading.

These notions conclude our examination of forex day trading, although learning never truly ends. Continue to research market linkages; they provide context for technical analysis. Success is achieved via continuous learning and adaptability.

Conclusion

The Path Forward

The journey of forex day trading reveals a world of limitless opportunities and constant growth. Technical analysis, risk management, psychology, and market wisdom all play a role in your trading journey. You'll gain skills necessary for long-term trading success by studying the concepts thoroughly and applying them practically.

Key Learning Integration.

Technical indicators are tools, not solutions. Years of market experience have taught me that combining multiple analysis methods results in more robust trading approaches.

Moving averages, momentum indicators, and volume analysis all work together to confirm trade opportunities. Understanding how different indicators complement one another is critical to success.

A Continuous Learning Approach

Markets evolve constantly, necessitating ongoing education and adaptation. My trading experiences demonstrate that successful traders never stop learning. You'll discover that each market phase provides new lessons and opportunities for growth. Trading journals and performance metrics should be reviewed on a regular basis to guide your development.

Strategy Evolution Process

Trading strategies must respond to changing market conditions. Through careful observation, I've noticed how strategies that work in trending markets frequently fail in ranging conditions. You'll learn how to adapt your strategy based on market conditions while adhering to sound risk management principles. Strategy refinement evolves into an ongoing process rather than a one-time task.

Professional development path

To achieve trading mastery, you must be dedicated and patient. My experience has taught me that structured learning and practical application lead to consistent improvement. You'll learn skills in stages, starting with strong fundamentals and progressing to more complex strategies. Each trading day provides opportunities to improve your craft.

Long-term Success Principles

Fundamental principles are essential for long-term trading success. Throughout market cycles, I've seen how disciplined traders keep profits while others struggle. You'll recognise that position sizing, risk management, and emotional control are more important than perfect entry points. These principles underpin all aspects of your trading journey.

Market Adaptation Techniques.

The flexibility of approach determines long-term survival. My trading history demonstrates how adapting to market changes ensures ongoing success. You will learn how to recognise market changes and adjust your strategies accordingly. This adaptability becomes your greatest asset in volatile forex markets.

Future Trade Development

The trading journey continues beyond these pages. Through ongoing market participation, I've learnt that mastery necessitates continuous growth. As your trading abilities improve, you will encounter new challenges and opportunities. Each achievement provides opportunities for advancement in your trading career.

Technical knowledge alone is insufficient for trading success. It requires combining multiple skills into a cohesive approach while maintaining emotional balance. Your journey entails ongoing learning, adaptation, and personal development. Maintain your commitment to your development while staying disciplined in the face of market challenges.

The concepts presented serve as a foundation for your trading future. Develop them through hands-on experience and ongoing research.

Your success is dependent on applying these principles consistently while remaining adaptable to market changes. Continue to improve your approach, learning from both successes and setbacks.

May your trading journey bring you both financial success and personal development. The road ahead provides limitless opportunities for those who approach markets with discipline, patience, and a commitment to continuous improvement. Applying these concepts in real market conditions is the first step towards trading success.

Video Access Page

Thank you for purchasing my book! As a token of my appreciation, I've made available exclusive video content just for you.

To access your complimentary videos, simply visit:

https://mega.nz/folder/IYZRQZTL#UIoA3WK6Gb_OfS2Xxq-iRA

Thank you for your support, and I hope these additional resources enhance your reading experience!

Best regards,

James willy

www.ingramcontent.com/pod-product-compliance
Lightning Source LLC
Chambersburg PA
CBHW071038240526
45469CB00006BD/2248